THIS
BOOK
belongs
To

ADVENTURES OF THE MAGICAL ORANGE BOOTS

#AOTMOB

THE WORLD'S FIRST CHILDREN'S BOOK
ILLUSTRATED BY YOU!!!

SEND
ILLUSTRATIONS 2:

art@magicalorangeboots.com

ART MATERIALS

COLORED PENCILS + CRAYONS - MARKERS + colored chalk glitter - oil pastels + paintbrushes

ILLUSTRATED BY:

YOU

Look MoM, I'M AN ILLUSTRATOR!!!

AWESOME IS POSSIBLE

WRITTEN BY:

HAKEEM
ANIMASHAUN

ADVENTURES OF THE MAGICAL ORANGE BOOTS

INTRODUCTION

A FORMAL PRESENTATION OF ONE PERSON TO ANOTHER,
IN WHICH EACH IS TOLD THE OTHER'S NAME; THE
START OF SOMETHING AWESOME

It's about 19 degrees outside in Washington, D.C. The snow is piled up to one's knees. Luckily, Little Levi is inside where the temperature is a nice 75. The only problem is...

He can't sleep!!!

Grandpa Joe and Grandma Nay are sitting on the world's most comfortable couch, just watching the time go away. Hot minty tea and a fireplace keep them from getting the goose bumps. Grandma Nay looks to her left and sees Little Levi rubbing his eyes.

Little Levi says, "I can't sleep. Read me a bedtime story pleassseee." Grandma Nay says, "Sorry little daredevil, I'm going to sleep." He sighs and looks down at his feet.

"Don't worry kido," Grandpa stands and says, "I'll tell you the coolest story of all time. Just need to find one thing." He pulls out a treasure chest that was hidden under the couch. Little Levi asks, "What's that for Grandpa?" He opens it and the room fills with bright orange lights!

Little Levi cannot believe his eyes and asks, "What's inside?" "It's something magical," Grandpa Joe replies, "It took me anywhere I wanted to go. It's simply awesome!" Little Levi fist pumps and jumps around in circles. "What is it, what is it, what is it!" Slowly taking it out, Grandpa Joe reveals a pair of bright awesome glowing magical orange boots.

Little Levi stares in amazement. "Whoa. What are those?" Grandpa Joe spins the boots around and whispers, "The NINE.2.SEVENS." Little Levi stomps his feet and covers his ears and even screams because he can't believe the magical orange boots have such a cool name.

NINE2
SEVEN

Grandpa Joe laughs and sets Little Levi on his knee. "Let me tell you the story of where it all began."

SEARCHING

CLOSELY LOOKING FOR SOMETHING OR SOMEONE THAT
MUST BE FOUND; SEEKING AWESOMENESS

"Today is my birthday and I'm going to turn up the volume on my favorite cartoon!" Joey said as he jumped out of bed and wiped the boogers out his eyes. He yawned as big as an alligator and stretched as wide as the sea. Joey dragged his feet all the way to the living room for a Yoo-Hoo chocolate flavored drink. He scratched his butt and recited the ABCs.

"Surprissseee!" his mother yelled. "Happy Birthday Joey! I made your favorite chocolate cake and got you a bunch of gifts!" Joey's eyes lit up. He loved getting new things, especially on his birthday. He ran straight to his mom and tackled her down to the ground like a sumo wrestler. "Thanks mama!"

Joey looked at his gifts and saw that they were as little as caterpillars. Then he looked closer and spotted the big golden box. He quickly ran to it but tripped. "Ouch." He got up to run but tripped again. "Double ouch." When he finally stopped tripping, he unwrapped the gifts.

Before he could see what was inside, his mother grabbed him and said, "It's time to eat!" Joey kicked and screamed and looked at her really mean.

His mother brought out the cake while singing, "Happy birthday to you...happy birthday to you...happy birthday dear Joey...happy birthday to yooouuu!"

Joey didn't look too happy.

His mother said, "Make a wish little troublemaker." Joey angrily replied, "I wish I could open the big golden box." She set the cake on the table, pointed at it and said, "Do you have any idea how long it took me to make that chocolate cake?" Joey said, "I don't care!" So he was sent to his room without eating anything.

Later that night...

Joey awoke on a mission to find the big golden box. As he opened his bedroom door, a loud screeching sound echoed throughout the house. He looked left and right to see if his mother was in sight. "Whoa, that was close." Then he tiptoed all the way to the living room in search of the big golden box.

#14

He looked around living room. He looked around the kitchen. He even looked around his ears. The big golden box was nowhere to be found, so Joey felt sad and laid out on the couch. For some reason it was harder than usual, so he looked underneath and guess what he found...

THE BIG GOLDEN BOX!

Joey opened the big golden box at the speed of light. To his
surprise, the room filled with bright orange lights! "Whoa."

Inside was a pair of bright awesome glowing magical orange boots and a note that read: Many magical adventures await you. Just close your eyes and say, 'Orange, A Place You Want To Go, and BOOM!' Joey quickly put on the boots, closed his eyes and...

Opened them back up. Joey couldn't think of anywhere to go. Then he remembered a place he learned about in school. It was a big gigantic desert filled with pyramids. "Orange! Egypt! BOOM!"

WISDOM

THE QUALITY OF HAVING EXPERIENCE, KNOWLEDGE, AND GOOD JUDGMENT; BEING AWESOMELY SMART

Joey opened his eyes to the sight of the sun. He looked all around but saw no one. He thought the world famous pyramids would be in plain sight. He looked confused as he stared down at his not so magical orange boots. "Where am I?"

Out of nowhere, a caravan of camels rushed toward him! Just seconds before the big bang, a longhaired ponytail girl came to the rescue and pulled him out the way. Joey said, "You just saved my life." She said, "You're welcome" and skipped away.

Joey brushed his shoulders off and caught up with her. He asked her how old she was. The longhaired ponytail girl used her fingers to count all the way up to 9. Joey said, "My teacher told me only grown ups could be heroes." She replied, "Nope. Kids could be too."

Joey didn't know what to believe so he asked her another question "Am I in Egypt?" She laughed and said, "Of course silly. You must have banged your head really hard. Where do you think you are?" Joey replied "Washington, D.C." She ran around in circles and asked a million questions "Have you seen the White House? Is it really big? Does the snow go all the way up to your knees?" Then she stopped and got suspicious. "Wait a minute. If you're supposed to be where the White House is, how did you end up in Egypt?"

Joey pointed at his boots. She looked confused and asked "Your shoes got you here?" Joey smiled and said, "I guess they're magical." She asked Joey if his boots had a name. She said, "It's good luck to name magical things." So Joey rubbed his chin and tried to think of a cool name.

Five minutes later...

still thinking.

Finally Joey said, "Okay, okay, okay I got it. Since you're 9 years old and I'm 7 years old we should bring them together and name my magical orange boots: The NINE.2.SEVENS!" The longhaired ponytail girl didn't say anything for about 5 seconds. Then she said, "I like it." Joey pumped his fists and chanted, "NINE.2.SEVEN! NINE.2.SEVEN! NINE.2.SEVEN!" The two laughed and began to walk northwest.

Joey asked her if she had a name. She laughed and replied, "Of course silly. Everybody has a name. Can you guess my name?" Joey took 3 guesses. "Is it Chloe? No...Zoe. Oh, I got it...its Guacamole." She laughed and said, "Guacamole is food. I'm a girl and my name is Nayla." Joey told her his name and they said nice to meet you at the same exact time.

#22

Joey yelled out, "JINX!" Nayla slapped his arm and said, "You beat me to it." Joey shrugged his shoulders and said, "Boys are faster than girls."

Nayla said, "No they're not." Joey said, "Yes we are." Nayla said, "No they're not." Joey said, "Yes we are." Nayla said, "Boys are slow." Joey said, "Boys are fast." Nayla said, "I bet I could beat you in a race." Joey laughed and said, "No you can't." Nayla said, "Lets race!" Joey said, "I'm not racing a girl." Nayla said, "You're scared a girl is going to beat you." Joey said, "No way." Nayla said, "Prove it." Joey said, "Okay, lets race."

Joey vs. Nayla

They drew two lines in the sand. One for the START and one for the FINSIH. Then they got in position. Joey raised a hand and said, "On your marks, get set..." and right before he could say the next word, Nayla screamed "GO!" She blew dust in Joey's face as she sprinted away. He huffed and puffed and tried to catch up. But he was too slow. Joey watched Nayla's long ponytail bounce up and down as she crossed the finish line. Nayla excitedly yelled, "I won! I won! Girls are faster than boys! Girls are faster than boys!"

Joey walked the other way. Nayla said, "Hey...wait. Where are you going?" Joey replied, "Away from you." Nayla put her hand on his shoulder and said, "Don't be such a sore loser." Joey turned to her and said, "You cheated." Nayla threw her hands in the air and said, "All is fair in love and war." Joey looked at her really mean.

Nayla said, "I'm sorry." Joey replied, "Apology not accepted," and walked away. Nayla cried "Oh c'mon. Don't be mad at me." Joey didn't say anything. Then she asked if he wanted to go on an adventure to the pyramids. Joey stopped walking and said, "I have to be home before it gets dark." Nayla frowned and made a puppy face. "But..." Joey hesitated, "I can go!" Nayla gave him a high five and the two began their journey to the world famous pyramids.

Along the way they met a big ole camel.

The camel said, "Cool boots buddy boy." Joey said, "Wow, you can talk." The camel replied, "My name is Christopher. What's your name?" Joey told the camel his name but Nayla remained silent. Christopher asked Joey if he would like to see the coolest pyramid of all time.

Nayla pulled Joey to the side before he could answer and said, "What are you doing? You know we shouldn't talk to strangers." Joey said, "But you just met me." Nayla replied, "Shhh. That's different, he's a freaking camel. I don't trust camels." They looked at him with detective eyes. Christopher looked as innocent as could be.

Joey said, "If we go I'll buy you ice cream." Nayla looked at the camel, then back at Joey, then back at the camel, then back at Joey. "Alright, alright, alright. What the heck. I'll go." Joey excitedly turned to Christopher and said, "Jolly good fellow, lead us to the coolest pyramid of all time!

The three traveled far and wide in the blazing hot sun. Joey had to sit down to catch his breath. He said, "It must be like infinity degrees." Nayla said, "You're too young to behave like a Grandpa," and pinched him on the arm. Joey cried out, "Ah! That hurt." Nayla replied, "Come on lets go! You're going to make me stomp my feet!" She began to stomp her feet. "STOMP! STOMP! STOMP! STOMP! STOMP!"

And continued to stomp her feet. "STOMP! STOMP! STOMP!"

She stopped stomping when she heard weird noises coming from behind the trees. The noises got louder and louder then suddenly stopped. A pack of big ole camels circled around them. Joey and Nayla got a little scared and said, "Hey Christopher, a little help here!" Christopher made the weird camel noise back, 'Nuuuuuurrr!' But it was no help, for it was 4 camels to 1.

#28

Then something crazy happened.

Christopher looked at Joey and Nayla and started to laugh "Hahahaha!" He joined the pack of camels and yelled out, "Didn't anyone ever tell you not to talk to strangers!"

The camels made weird noise, after weird noise, after weird noise. Christopher stretched his camel head up high and said, "Lead them to the evilest pyramid of all time!" Nayla cried out, "What are you going to do to us?" Christopher screamed, "Silence! You'll soon find out."

The evilest pyramid of all time was guarded by a mini camel. His body was small but his head was gigantic, so he wore a big ole hat to cover it up. Joey and Nayla were shaking and had the goose bumps. Christopher joked with the mini camel and asked, "What do you think we should do with them?" The mini camel replied, "Tie them up and feed them to the dogs." The two laughed hysterically and kicked Joey and Nayla into the pyramid.

Joey and Nayla looked around and saw bones, bugs, and bats. Christopher shoved them onto slimy smelly chairs and tied Nayla's hands and legs.

Christopher looked at Joey and said, "Remember the caravan of camels that almost crushed you. If it weren't for your little girlfriend you would have been dead meat. Anyway, I was the camel in front. I saw your boots glow and thought they were magical or something. So I followed you and your little girlfriend around. Then lured you here to my evil pyramid! Big pat on my back, how you like me now?" Joey stopped listening after Christopher said magical. The word reminded him that his boots were magical. He could escape with Nayla. They could get away!

Joey looked at Nayla and whispered, "I have a plan." Nayla asked, "What is it?" Joey replied, "My boots. They are magical remember. We could..." Christopher butted in and asked, "What are you two whispering about?" Joey quickly said, "Nothing." Christopher made his way over to him and began to tie his hands. "It's your turn now buddy boy." Joey knew he had to do something quick before it was too late.

Joey coughed, "Uh, uh, uh, uh." Christopher lifted his big head to see what was going on. That spared Joey about 10 seconds. Christopher's head was really big. Joey looked at Nayla one last time and whispered, "I'll come back for you." He closed his eyes as a single tear rolled down his face and yelled with all his might "Orange, China, BOOM!"

And just like that, he was gone.

COURAGE

THE ABILITY TO DO SOMETHING THAT FRIGHTENS YOU;
MAKING AWESOME HAPPEN EVEN WHEN YOU'RE
REALLY SCARED

It was a warm but cloudy afternoon on the streets of Shanghai. Joey wandered around China with an upside down smile. He looked at the sky and almost cried. Before the tears fell down his face, he spotted a fiery red dragon out the corner of his eye. It got closer and closer and Joey realized...

It was coming right at him!

Joey quickly tried to run but tripped. "Ouch." He got up and ran fast but the dragon was faster and crash-landed at his feet. Joey closed his eyes and dropped down to his knees.

The dragon had yellow nasty smelly teeth. It smelled so bad it made Joey sneeze. "Ah-Choo!" He had no choice but to open his eyes and face his demise.

To Joey's surprise, the dragon did not swallow him up. Instead it smiled and said, "Hello little guy. I'm Bao the dragon." Joey screamed, "Ahhh!" and ran like crazy.

He just ran, he ran so far away, he ran all around the streets of Shanghai but couldn't get away.

Bao said, "Hey! Why are you running from me?" Joey replied,
"Because you're scary." Bao laughed and said, "Looks could be
deceiving. I am not what I appear to be." Joey took two steps back.
He didn't want to trust another stranger.

Bao took a deep breath and told Joey a story. "Once upon a time, there lived a little dragon who was afraid of everything. But his whole life changed in one day. He realized he had a choice: be courageous or live in fear. What do you think he chose to do?"

Joey said, "Face his fears." Bao replied, "Exactly! Now he gets to eat all the ice cream he wants." Joey laughed and asked Bao if he was the little dragon. Bao sat down next to Joey and said, "Yes. But now I'm the brave hearted dragon. There's a big difference."

Joey told Bao all about the NINE.2.SEVENS, Nayla, and everything
that happened in Egypt. Bao asked Joey what he was going to do.
Joey said, "I don't know. I guess I have to go back and save Nayla."
Bao said, "Yes. But say it like you mean it!" Joey cleared his throat
and said, "I will face my fears and save Nayla." Bao yelled out,
"Louder!" Joey screamed, "I will face my fears and save Nayla!"
Bao wasn't impressed and yelled out, "Louder! Make me believe it!"
Joey jumped and yelled at the top of his lungs, "I must face my
fears! I must face my fears! I must face my fears and save Nayla!"

Bao excitedly blew fire in the sky. Joey took two steps back, closed his eyes and screamed "Orange, Egypt, BOOM!"

COMPASSION

CONCERN FOR THE SUFFERINGS OR MISFORTUNES
OF OTHERS; HELPING PEOPLE BECOME AWESOME
LIKE YOU

The journey to the evilest pyramid of all time was long and Joey wanted to take a break. He thought about the words of wisdom he learned from Bao. Be courageous or live in fear. Be courageous or live in fear. He repeated it to himself over and over. As Joey got closer to the evilest pyramid of all time, he heard camel voices. He hid behind a tree and peaked to see who it was.

It was the mini camel with the big ole hat dancing around in circles and singing "Oh I just can't wait to be king!" Joey grabbed the stick and whispered to himself "This is it." He turned around and struck the mini camel with all his might.

Joey entered the pyramid and saw four camels cart Nayla off to the back. There was no time to think, he just had to attack. He screamed, "Leave her alone!" and charged like a maniac.

Joey took down three camels but there was one left. It began to make the weird loud camel noise like crazy "Nuuuurrrr!" Joey was out of rocks. He didn't know what to do. Nayla yelled, "Use the stick!" as the camel leaped toward Joey.

Joey quickly lifted the stick and struck the camel before it could bite. "Joey!" Nayla cried out, "Are you okay?" He stumbled away from the camels and helped untie her from the slimy smelly chair. They gave each other a big hug. Joey said, "I told you I would come back."

Suddenly Christopher The Camel appeared from the corner and said, "You fool, you've come back to save your friend with only a stick. I've got bones that are bigger than that!" Joey replied, "Who said all I came with is a stick!" All of a sudden, Bao The Dragon blew fire in the sky and said, "You evil camel. Pick on someone your own size!" Christopher said, "As you wish. Let the games begin!"

Bao The Dragon vs. Christopher The Camel

Christopher threw the first blow that took Bao down to the ground.

Christopher yelled, "You're just a dragon, you can't defeat me!"

The two wrestled on the ground then finally got back on their feet.

Christopher said, "Is that all you got!" and struck again. This time

Bao was ready.

Bao did a 360 spin and blew a big fat fireball right at Christopher. Bao screamed, "Take that! Take that!" Christopher cried out, "Ahhhhhhhh!" and ran off waging his BBQ'd tail.

The sun shined bright on Joey and Nayla as they walked outside. Bao stayed behind and closed the gates to the evilest pyramid of all time.

Nayla asked, "How did you get a dragon to come to Egypt?" Joey replied, "I have my ways," and waved to the dragon. Bao waved his lumpy claws in reply. Joey said, "I met him in China. He taught me a lot of cool things." Nayla looked a little jealous and asked, "Oh yeah, like what?" Joey sat down and said, "Well wisdom because little kids should not talk to strangers. Courage because sometimes you just have to do what you're afraid of. And compassion because..." Joey couldn't think of what to say so he spoke from the heart.

"I think I love you."

There was complete silence for like infinity. Joey got a little nervous and was about to speak, but luckily Bao butted in between and said, "Lets all get ice cream!"

They chased down a Mister Softee truck yelling, "Ice cream! Ice cream!" Nayla got strawberry shortcake and Joey got OREO cookies and cream. Bao got mint flavor ice cream and blew fire on it that turned it into hot minty tea. Nayla laughed and said, "You're so crazy."

#50

51

Joey, Nayla, and Bao ate ice cream as they watched the sunset. It was a really beautiful scene. Joey said, "This is awesome." Nayla smiled and said, "I'm a luckiest girl in the world." Bao cried out, "I think I just burned my tongue." They all laughed.

Bao got in a four-point stance and told Joey and Nayla to hop on his back. Joey jumped on but Nayla stayed behind. Joey said, "C'mon, hop on." Nayla cried out, "I'm scared." Bao said, "I'm a pretty safe flyer." Joey reached out his hand to her and said, "Be courageous or live in fear." Nayla crossed her arms and looked away. Joey padded Bao on the back to fly off. Nayla yelled out "Wait!" Joey smiled and said, "You only live once." Nayla said, "Alright, alright, alright. Here goes nothing." She jumped on as Bao blew fire in the sky and flew off.

#52

From a thousand feet above, they finally got to see the world famous pyramids. Joey and Nayla said, "Awesome is possible" at the same time. Joey yelled, "JINX!" He raised his hands in victory and said, "I told you boys are faster than girls." Nayla pinched his arm and laughed.

They crash landed in front of Nayla's house knocking over the mailbox. Bao said, "Oops." Joey said, "It's been a fun day." Nayla replied, "Thanks for everything." Joey smiled and taught Nayla their new handshake. They repeated it in unison. "Pound it, bring it back, slap."

Nayla asked Joey if he wanted to know a secret. He said yes and she made him close his eyes and count to five. Nayla whispered, "I think I love you too" and kissed Joey on the cheek. She skipped away and said, "See you later alligator." Joey's boots shined bright like a diamond.

Joey jumped for joy! On his very first adventure, he had fallen in love.

He knew exactly where to go. "Orange, Home, BOOM!"

Joey rushed to his room and got in bed. His mother opened the door and asked if he was still awake. Joey pretended to be asleep. His mother kissed him goodnight and told him that she loved him. Once she closed the door, he opened his eyes to the shine of the orange boots. "Whoa. They really are magical." Joey closed his eyes and drifted off into sleep.

FINDING

THE ACTION OF DISCOVERING SOMEONE OR
SOMETHING; THAT AWESOME MOMENT WHEN
EVERYTHING BECOMES CLEAR

Grandpa Joe smiles as he finishes telling the story of the magical orange boots. He looks down to see Little Levi falling asleep. Grandpa Joe tucks him into bed and says goodnight.

In the morning, Little Levi awakes to a bright orange glow coming from his feet. He jumps out of bed and guess what he sees...

The bright awesome glowing magical orange boots.
The NINE.2.SEVENS!

He's so excited he runs to the living room and looks for Grandpa
Joe. He looks all around but he is nowhere to be found.

Grandma Nay appears in the hallway and asks, "What's all the fuss about?" Little Levi runs to her and yells, "My boots, my boots, Grandma look at my boots!" She looks down at his boots and says, "Now isn't that magical." Little Levi says, "Yes, yes they are. Where's Grandpa. I want to show him." She replies, "He's sleeping Levi. But he wanted me to give you this." Grandma Nay hands Little Levi a note and kisses him on the cheek.

Little Levi runs to his room but trips and falls. "Ouch!" He reads the note to cheer him up. "Many magical adventures await you. Just close your eyes and say: Orange, A Place You Want To Go, and BOOM!"

Little Levi jumps up and yells out with all his mighty might "Orange, Hollywood, BOOM!"

And with that,

Adventures of the Magical Orange Boots live on forever...

and ever...

and ever!

ADVENTURES OF THE MAGICAL ORANGE BOOTS

WRITTEN BY: HAKEEM ANIMASHAUN

AUTHOR'S NOTE

Hakeem Animashaun was born on March 12, 1991. With him being a Pisces and all, he spends half of the day in a dream world and the other half in reality.

It just so happened that he was in one of his "dreams" on the day he found the ORANGE BOOTS, while shopping at a local thrift store in Los Angeles, CA. The moment he laid eyes on them he knew they were magical. He had to have them! So he paid the man behind the register the money and drove back home.

It was 6:12pm and there was tons of traffic. He didn't mind, he just plugged in his iPod and sang along to 'Miguel – Adorn' all the way home. When he finally made it home, the sun had set and it was about 7:45pm.

He put on his favorite movie, but that was too slow. He read his favorite book, but that couldn't keep his attention. He called some friends, but all their conversations got boring. He looked at his ORANGE BOOTS and saw dirt on them. He grabbed a toothbrush and soap. By the time he finished cleaning it was 8:45pm. A whole hour had passed and he remembered that his favorite show was coming on at 9:30pm.

AUTHOR'S NOTE cont.

Hakeem wanted snacks for the show so he went to the grocery store to pick up some OREOS. He walked down at least 7 aisles but none of them had what he was looking for. He looked at his watch: 9:05pm. It was only 25 minutes till show time so he had to hurry up. He turned down aisle 1 and saw two store employees. Just the help he needed! They said he could find it on aisle 3. He thanked them and ran down the aisle, but tripped on a basket lying on the floor. The food scattered everywhere!

He quickly got up to help pick up the items. To his surprise, a pack of OREOS was on the floor. He reached out for it and touched hands with the most beautiful girl he had ever seen. They locked eyes for what seemed like infinity.

He asked the beautiful girl if the OREOS were hers. She nodded her head in agreement then lifted an orange boot and asked if it was his. He looked down and was missing a shoe! All he could do was laugh. She told him that she had actually been looking for ORANGE BOOTS to use at a photo shoot the next day. He told her that he had actually been looking for OREOS to eat while watching his favorite show.

They smiled at each other. What a coincidence. He looked at the time: 9:27pm.

THANK YOU

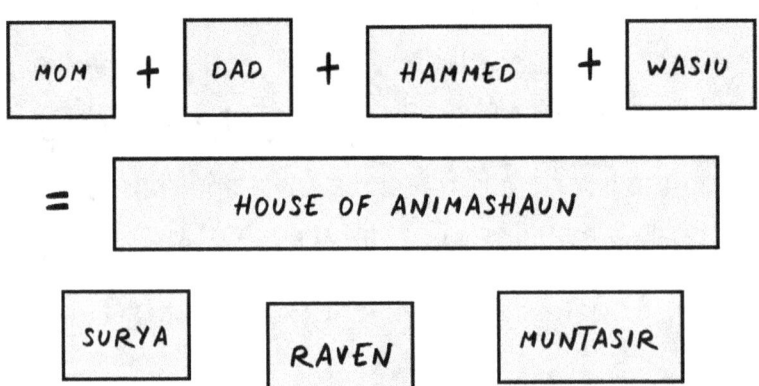

MOM + DAD + HAMMED + WASIU

= HOUSE OF ANIMASHAUN

SURYA   RAVEN   MUNTASIR

AWESOME IS POSSIBLE